POEMS.

BY

BRET HARTE.

BOSTON:
JAMES R. OSGOOD AND COMPANY,
LATE TICKNOR & FIELDS, AND FIELDS, OSGOOD, & CO.
1871.

UNIVERSITY PRESS: WELCH, BIGELOW, & CO.,
CAMBRIDGE.

CONTENTS.

SAN FRANCISCO.

FROM THE SEA.

SERENE, indifferent of Fate,
Thou sittest at the Western Gate ;

Upon thy heights so lately won
Still slant the banners of the sun ;

Thou seest the white seas strike their tents,
O Warder of two Continents !

And scornful of the peace that flies
Thy angry winds and sullen skies,

Thou drawest all things, small or great,
To thee, beside the Western Gate.

* * * * *

O lion's whelp, that hidest fast
In jungle growth of spire and mast,

I know thy cunning and thy greed,
Thy hard high lust and wilful deed,

And all thy glory loves to tell
Of specious gifts material.

Drop down, O fleecy Fog, and hide
Her sceptic sneer, and all her pride!

Wrap her, O Fog, in gown and hood
Of her Franciscan Brotherhood.

Hide me her faults, her sin and blame;
With thy gray mantle cloak her shame!

So shall she, cowléd, sit and pray
Till morning bears her sins away.

Then rise, O fleecy Fog, and raise
The glory of her coming days;

Be as the cloud that flecks the seas
Above her smoky argosies.

When forms familiar shall give place
To stranger speech and newer face;

When all her throes and anxious fears
Lie hushed in the repose of years;

When Art shall raise and Culture lift
The sensual joys and meaner thrift,

And all fulfilled the vision, we
Who watch and wait shall never see,—

Who, in the morning of her race,
Toiled fair or meanly in our place,—

But, yielding to the common lot,
Lie unrecorded and forgot.

THE ANGELUS,

HEARD AT THE MISSION DOLORES, 1868.

BELLS of the Past, whose long-forgotten music
Still fills the wide expanse,
Tingeing the sober twilight of the Present
With color of romance:

I hear your call, and see the sun descending
On rock and wave and sand,
As down the coast the Mission voices blending
Girdle the heathen land.

Within the circle of your incantation
No blight nor mildew falls;

Nor fierce unrest, nor lust, nor low ambition
Passes those airy walls.

Borne on the swell of your long waves receding,
I touch the farther Past, —
I see the dying glow of Spanish glory,
The sunset dream and last!

Before me rise the dome-shaped Mission towers,
The white Presidio;
The swart commander in his leathern jerkin,
The priest in stole of snow.

Once more I see Portala's cross uplifting
Above the setting sun;
And past the headland, northward, slowly drifting
The freighted galleon.

O solemn bells! whose consecrated masses
　　Recall the faith of old, —
O tinkling bells! that lulled with twilight music
　　The spiritual fold!

Your voices break and falter in the darkness, —
　　Break, falter, and are still;
And veiled and mystic, like the Host descending,
　　The sun sinks from the hill!

THE MOUNTAIN HEART'S-EASE.

BY scattered rocks and turbid waters shifting,
By furrowed glade and dell,
To feverish men thy calm, sweet face uplifting,
Thou stayest them to tell

The delicate thought, that cannot find expression,
For ruder speech too fair,
That, like thy petals, trembles in possession,
And scatters on the air.

The miner pauses in his rugged labor,
And, leaning on his spade,

Laughingly calls unto his comrade-neighbor
To see thy charms displayed;

But in his eyes a mist unwonted rises,
And for a moment clear,
Some sweet home face his foolish thought surprises
And passes in a tear, —

Some boyish vision of his Eastern village,
Of uneventful toil,
Where golden harvests followed quiet tillage
Above a peaceful soil:

One moment only, for the pick, uplifting,
Through root and fibre cleaves,
And on the muddy current slowly drifting
Are swept thy bruiséd leaves.

And yet, O poet, in thy homely fashion,
Thy work thou dost fulfil,
For on the turbid current of his passion
Thy face is shining still!

GRIZZLY.

COWARD, — of heroic size,
In whose lazy muscles lies
Strength we fear and yet despise;
Savage, — whose relentless tusks
Are content with acorn husks;
Robber, — whose exploits ne'er soared
O'er the bee's or squirrel's hoard;
Whiskered chin, and feeble nose,
Claws of steel on baby toes, —
Here, in solitude and shade,

Shambling, shuffling, plantigrade,
Be thy courses undismayed!

Here, where Nature makes thy bed,
Let thy rude, half-human tread
  Point to hidden Indian springs,
Lost in ferns and fragrant grasses,
  Hovered o'er by timid wings,
Where the wood-duck lightly passes,
Where the wild bee holds her sweets, —
Epicurean retreats,
Fit for thee, and better than
Fearful spoils of dangerous man.

In thy fat-jowled deviltry
Friar Tuck shall live in thee;
Thou mayst levy tithe and dole;
  Thou shalt spread the woodland cheer,

From the pilgrim taking toll;
  Match thy cunning with his fear;
Eat, and drink, and have thy fill;
Yet remain an outlaw still!

MADROÑO.

CAPTAIN of the Western wood,
Thou that apest Robin Hood!
Green above thy scarlet hose,
How thy velvet mantle shows;
Never tree like thee arrayed,
O thou gallant of the glade!

When the fervid August sun
Scorches all it looks upon,
And the balsam of the pine
Drips from stem to needle fine,
Round thy compact shade arranged,
Not a leaf of thee is changed!

When the yellow autumn sun
Saddens all it looks upon,
Spreads its sackcloth on the hills,
Strews its ashes in the rills,
Thou thy scarlet hose dost doff,
And in limbs of purest buff
Challengest the sombre glade
For a sylvan masquerade.

Where, O where, shall he begin
Who would paint thee, Harlequin?
With thy waxen burnished leaf,
With thy branches' red relief,
With thy poly-tinted fruit,
In thy spring or autumn suit, —
Where begin, and O, where end, —
Thou whose charms all art transcend?

COYOTE.

BLOWN out of the prairie in twilight and dew,
Half bold and half timid, yet lazy all through;
Loath ever to leave, and yet fearful to stay,
He limps in the clearing, — an outcast in gray.

A shade on the stubble, a ghost by the wall,
Now leaping, now limping, now risking a fall,
Lop-eared and large-jointed, but ever alway
A thoroughly vagabond outcast in gray.

Here, Carlo, old fellow, — he's one of your kind, —
Go, seek him, and bring him in out of the wind.

What! snarling, my Carlo! So — even dogs may
Deny their own kin in the outcast in gray.

Well, take what you will, — though it be on the sly,
Marauding, or begging, — I shall not ask why;
But will call it a dole, just to help on his way
A four-footed friar in orders of gray!

TO A SEA-BIRD.

SANTA CRUZ, 1869.

SAUNTERING hither on listless wings,
Careless vagabond of the sea,
Little thou heedest the surf that sings,
The bar that thunders, the shale that rings,—
Give me to keep thy company.

Little thou hast, old friend, that 's new,
Storms and wrecks are old things to thee;
Sick am I of these changes, too;
Little to care for, little to rue,—
I on the shore, and thou on the sea.

All of thy wanderings, far and near,
  Bring thee at last to shore and me;
All of my journeyings end them here,
This our tether must be our cheer, —
  I on the shore, and thou on the sea.

Lazily rocking on ocean's breast,
  Something in common, old friend, have we;
Thou on the shingle seek'st thy nest,
I to the waters look for rest, —
  I on the shore, and thou on the sea.

HER LETTER.

I'M sitting alone by the fire,
Dressed just as I came from the dance,
In a robe even *you* would admire, —
It cost a cool thousand in France;
I 'm be-diamonded out of all reason,
My hair is done up in a cue:
In short, sir, "the belle of the season"
Is wasting an hour on you.

A dozen engagements I 've broken;
I left in the midst of a set;

Likewise a proposal, half spoken,
  That waits — on the stairs — for me yet.
They say he 'll be rich, — when he grows up, —
  And then he adores me indeed.
And you, sir, are turning your nose up,
  Three thousand miles off, as you read.

"And how do I like my position?"
  "And what do I think of New York?"
"And now, in my higher ambition,
  With whom do I waltz, flirt, or talk?"
"And is n't it nice to have riches,
  And diamonds and silks, and all that?"
"And are n't it a change to the ditches
  And tunnels of Poverty Flat?"

Well, yes, — if you saw us out driving
  Each day in the park, four-in-hand, —

If you saw poor dear mamma contriving
  To look supernaturally grand, —
If you saw papa's picture, as taken
  By Brady, and tinted at that, —
You 'd never suspect he sold bacon
  And flour at Poverty Flat.

And yet, just this moment, when sitting
  In the glare of the grand chandelier, —
In the bustle and glitter befitting
  The "finest *soirée* of the year," —
In the mists of a *gaze de Chambéry*,
  And the hum of the smallest of talk, —
Somehow, Joe, I thought of the "Ferry,"
  And the dance that we had on "The Fork";

Of Harrison's barn, with its muster
  Of flags festooned over the wall;

Of the candles that shed their soft lustre
  And tallow on head-dress and shawl;
Of the steps that we took to one fiddle;
  Of the dress of my queer *vis-à-vis;*
And how I once went down the middle
  With the man that shot Sandy McGee;

Of the moon that was quietly sleeping
  On the hill, when the time came to go;
Of the few baby peaks that were peeping
  From under their bedclothes of snow;
Of that ride,— that to me was the rarest;
  Of — the something you said at the gate
Ah, Joe, then I was n't an heiress
  To "the best-paying lead in the State."

Well, well, it 's all past; yet it 's funny
  To think, as I stood in the glare

Of fashion and beauty and money,
  That I should be thinking, right there,
Of some one who breasted high water,
  And swam the North Fork, and all that,
Just to dance with old Folinsbee's daughter,
  The Lily of Poverty Flat.

But goodness! what nonsense I 'm writing!
  (Mamma says my taste still is low,)
Instead of my triumphs reciting,
  I 'm spooning on Joseph, — heigh-ho!
And I 'm to be "finished" by travel, —
  Whatever 's the meaning of that, —
O, why did papa strike pay gravel
  In drifting on Poverty Flat?

Good night, — here 's the end of my paper;
  Good night, — if the longitude please, —

For maybe, while wasting my taper,
  Your sun 's climbing over the trees.
But know, if you have n't got riches,
  And are poor, dearest Joe, and all that,
That my heart 's somewhere there in the ditches,
  And you 've struck it, — on Poverty Flat.

DICKENS IN CAMP.

ABOVE the pines the moon was slowly drifting,
    The river sang below;
The dim Sierras, far beyond, uplifting
    Their minarets of snow.

The roaring camp-fire, with rude humor, painted
    The ruddy tints of health
On haggard face and form that drooped and fainted
    In the fierce race for wealth;

Till one arose, and from his pack's scant treasure
    A hoarded volume drew,

And cards were dropped from hands of listless
leisure
To hear the tale anew;

And then, while round them shadows gathered
faster,
And as the firelight fell,
He read aloud the book wherein the Master
Had writ of "Little Nell."

Perhaps 't was boyish fancy, — for the reader
Was youngest of them all, —
But, as he read, from clustering pine and cedar
A silence seemed to fall;

The fir-trees, gathering closer in the shadows,
Listened in every spray,

While the whole camp, with "Nell" on English
meadows,
Wandered and lost their way.

And so in mountain solitudes — o'ertaken
As by some spell divine —
Their cares dropped from them like the needles
shaken
From out the gusty pine.

Lost is that camp, and wasted all its fire:
And he who wrought that spell? —
Ah, towering pine and stately Kentish spire,
Ye have one tale to tell!

Lost is that camp! but let its fragrant story
Blend with the breath that thrills

With hop-vines' incense all the pensive glory
 That fills the Kentish hills.

And on that grave where English oak and holly
 And laurel wreaths intwine,
Deem it not all a too presumptuous folly, —
 This spray of Western pine!

July, 1870.

WHAT THE ENGINES SAID.

OPENING OF THE PACIFIC RAILROAD.

WHAT was it the Engines said,
Pilots touching, — head to head
Facing on the single track,
Half a world behind each back?
This is what the Engines said,
Unreported and unread!

With a prefatory screech,
In a florid Western speech,
Said the Engine from the WEST:
"I am from Sierra's crest;

And, if altitude 's a test,
Why, I reckon, it 's confessed,
That I 've done my level best."

Said the Engine from the EAST:
"They who work best talk the least.
S'pose you whistle down your brakes;
What you 've done is no great shakes,—
Pretty fair,—but let our meeting
Be a different kind of greeting.
Let these folks with champagne stuffing,
Not their Engines, do the *puffing*.

"Listen! Where Atlantic beats
Shores of snow and summer heats;
Where the Indian autumn skies
Paint the woods with wampum dyes,

I have chased the flying sun,
Seeing all he looked upon,
Blessing all that he has blest,
Nursing in my iron breast
All his vivifying heat,
All his clouds about my crest;
And before my flying feet
Every shadow must retreat."

Said the Western Engine, "Phew!"
And a long low whistle blew.
"Come now, really that's the oddest
Talk for one so very modest, —
You brag of your East! *You* do?
Why, *I* bring the East to *you!*
All the Orient, all Cathay,
Find through me the shortest way,

And the sun you follow here
Rises in my hemisphere.
Really, — if one must be rude, —
Length, my friend, ain't longitude."

Said the Union, "Don't reflect, or
I 'll run over some Director."
Said the Central, "I 'm Pacific,
But, when riled, I 'm quite terrific.
Yet to-day we shall not quarrel,
Just to show these folks this moral,
How two Engines — in their vision —
Once have met without collision."

That is what the Engines said,
Unreported and unread;
Spoken slightly through the nose,
With a whistle at the close.

"THE RETURN OF BELISARIUS."

MUD FLAT, 1860.

SO you 're back from your travels, old fellow,
  And you left but a twelvemonth ago;
You 've hobnobbed with Louis Napoleon,
  Eugenie, and kissed the Pope's toe.
By Jove, it is perfectly stunning,
  Astounding, — and all that, you know;
Yes, things are about as you left them
  In Mud Flat a twelvemonth ago.

The boys! — They 're all right, — Oh! Dick Ashley,
  He 's buried somewhere in the snow;

He was lost on the Summit, last winter,
  And Bob has a hard row to hoe.
You knew that he 's got the consumption?
  You did n't! Well, come, that 's a go;
I certainly wrote you at Baden, —
  Dear me! that was six months ago.

I got all your outlandish letters,
  All stamped by some foreign P. O.
I handed myself to Miss Mary
  That sketch of a famous château.
Tom Saunders is living at 'Frisco, —
  They say that he cuts quite a show.
You did n't meet Euchre-deck Billy
  Anywhere on your road to Cairo?

So you thought of the rusty old cabin,
  The pines, and the valley below;

And heard the North Fork of the Yuba,
  As you stood on the banks of the Po?
'T was just like your romance, old fellow;
  But now there is standing a row
Of stores on the site of the cabin
  That you lived in a twelvemonth ago.

But it's jolly to see you, old fellow, —
  To think it's a twelvemonth ago!
And you have seen Louis Napoleon,
  And look like a Johnny Crapaud.
Come in. You will surely see Mary, —
  You know we are married. What, no? —
O, ay. I forgot there was something
  Between you a twelvemonth ago.

"TWENTY YEARS."

BEG your pardon, old fellow! I think
I was dreaming just now, when you spoke.
The fact is, the musical clink
Of the ice on your wine-goblet's brink
A chord of my memory woke.

And I stood in the pasture-field where
Twenty summers ago I had stood;
And I heard in that sound, I declare,
The clinkings of bells on the air,
Of the cows coming home from the wood.

Then the apple-blooms shook on the hill;
And the mullein-stalks tilted each lance;
And the sun behind Rapalye's mill
Was my uttermost West, and could thrill
Like some fanciful land of romance.

Then my friend was a hero, and then
My girl was an angel. In fine,
I drank buttermilk; for at ten
Faith asks less to aid her, than when
At thirty we doubt over wine.

Ah well, it *does* seem that I must
Have been dreaming just now when you spoke,
Or lost, very like, in the dust
Of the years that slow fashioned the crust
On that bottle whose seal you last broke.

Twenty years was its age, did you say?
Twenty years? Ah, my friend, it is true!
All the dreams that have flown since that day,
All the hopes in that time passed away,
Old friend, I've been drinking with you!

FATE.

"THE sky is clouded, the rocks are bare;
The spray of the tempest is white in air;
The winds are out with the waves at play,
And I shall not tempt the sea to-day.

"The trail is narrow, the wood is dim,
The panther clings to the arching limb;
And the lion's whelps are abroad at play,
And I shall not join in the chase to-day."

But the ship sailed safely over the sea,
And the hunters came from the chase in glee;
And the town that was builded upon a rock
Was swallowed up in the earthquake shock.

IN DIALECT.

"JIM."

SAY there! P'r'aps
  Some on you chaps
 Might know Jim Wild?
Well, — no offence:
Thar ain't no sense
 In gittin' riled!

Jim was my chum
 Up on the Bar:
That 's why I come
 Down from up yar,
Lookin' for Jim.
Thank ye, sir! *You*

Ain't of that crew, —
  Blest if you are!

Money? — Not much:
  That ain't my kind:
I ain't no such.
  Rum? — I don't mind,
Seein' it 's you.

Well, this yer Jim,
Did you know him? —
Jess 'bout your size;
Same kind of eyes? —
Well, that is strange:
  Why, it 's two year
  Since he came here,
Sick, for a change.

Well, here 's to us:
    Eh?
The h—— you say!
    Dead?—
That little cuss?

What makes you star,—
You over thar?
Can't a man drop
's glass in yer shop
But you must rar'?
  It would n't take
  D—— much to break
You and your bar.

    Dead!
Poor — little — Jim!

— Why, thar was me,
Jones, and Bob Lee,
Harry and Ben, —
No-account men:
Then to take *him!*

Well, thar — Good by, —
No more, sir, — I —
        Eh?
What's that you say? —
Why, dern it! — sho! —
No? Yes! By Jo!
        Sold!
Sold! Why, you limb,
You ornery,
        Derned old
Long-legged Jim!

CHIQUITA.

BEAUTIFUL! Sir, you may say so. Thar is n't her match in the county.
Is thar, old gal, — Chiquita, my darling, my beauty?
Feel of that neck, sir, — thar 's velvet! Whoa! Steady, — ah, will you, you vixen!
Whoa! I say. Jack, trot her out; let the gentleman look at her paces.

Morgan! — She ain't nothin' else, and I 've got the papers to prove it.
Sired by Chippewa Chief, and twelve hundred dollars won't buy her.

Briggs of Tuolumne owned her. Did you know
Briggs of Tuolumne ? —
Busted hisself in White Pine, and blew out his
brains down in 'Frisco ?

Hed n't no savey — hed Briggs. Thar, Jack !
that 'll do, — quit that foolin' !
Nothin' to what she kin do, when she 's got her
work cut out before her.
Hosses is hosses, you know, and likewise, too,
jockeys is jockeys ;
And 't ain't ev'ry man as can ride as knows what
a hoss has got in him.

Know the old ford on the Fork, that nearly got
Flanigan's leaders ?
Nasty in daylight, you bet, and a mighty rough
ford in low water !

Well, it ain't six weeks ago that me and the
Jedge and his nevey
Struck for that ford in the night, in the rain, and
the water all round us;

Up to our flanks in the gulch, and Rattlesnake
Creek just a bilin',
Not a plank left in the dam, and nary a bridge
on the river.
I had the gray, and the Jedge had his roan, and
his nevey, Chiquita;
And after us trundled the rocks jest loosed from
the top of the cañon.

Lickity, lickity, switch, we came to the ford, and
Chiquita
Buckled right down to her work, and afore I
could yell to her rider,

Took water jest at the ford, and there was the
Jedge and me standing,
And twelve hundred dollars of hoss-flesh afloat,
and a driftin' to thunder!

Would ye b'lieve it? that night that hoss, that ar'
filly, Chiquita,
Walked herself into her stall, and stood there, all
quiet and dripping:
Clean as a beaver or rat, with nary a buckle of
harness,
Just as she swam the Fork, — that hoss, that ar'
filly, Chiquita.

That's what I call a hoss! and — What did you
say? — O, the nevey?
Drownded, I reckon, — leastways, he never kem
back to deny it.

Ye see the derned fool had no seat,—ye could n't
have made him a rider;
And then, ye know, boys will be boys, and hosses
—well, hosses is hosses!

DOW'S FLAT.

1856.

DOW'S FLAT. That 's its name.
And I reckon that you
Are a stranger? The same?
Well, I thought it was true,—
For thar is n't a man on the river as can't spot the place at first view.

It was called after Dow,—
Which the same was an ass,—
And as to the how
Thet the thing kem to pass,—
Jest tie up your hoss to that buckeye, and sit ye down here in the grass:

You see this 'yer Dow
  Hed the worst kind of luck;
He slipped up somehow
  On each thing thet he struck.
Why, ef he 'd a straddled thet fence-rail the derned
    thing 'ed get up and buck.

He mined on the bar
  Till he could n't pay rates;
He was smashed by a car
  When he tunnelled with Bates;
And right on the top of his trouble kem his wife
    and five kids from the States.

It was rough, — mighty rough;
  But the boys they stood by,
And they brought him the stuff
  For a house, on the sly;

And the old woman,—well, she did washing, and
took on when no one was nigh.

But this yer luck of Dow's
Was so powerful mean
That the spring near his house
Dried right up on the green;
And he sunk forty feet down for water, but nary
a drop to be seen.

Then the bar petered out,
And the boys would n't stay;
And the chills got about,
And his wife fell away;
But Dow, in his well, kept a peggin' in his usual
ridikilous way.

One day,—it was June,—
And a year ago, jest,—

This Dow kem at noon
To his work like the rest,
With a shovel and pick on his shoulder, and a derringer hid in his breast.

He goes to the well,
And he stands on the brink,
And stops for a spell
Jest to listen and think:
For the sun in his eyes, (jest like this, sir!) you see, kinder made the cuss blink.

His two ragged gals
In the gulch were at play,
And a gownd that was Sal's
Kinder flapped on a bay:
Not much for a man to be leavin', but his all, — as I 've heer'd the folks say.

And — That 's a peart hoss
 Thet you 've got, — ain't it now?
What might be her cost?
 Eh? Oh! — Well, then, Dow —
Let 's see, — well, that forty-foot grave was n't his,
 sir, that day, anyhow.

For a blow of his pick
 Sorter caved in the side,
And he looked and turned sick,
 Then he trembled and cried.
For you see the dern cuss had struck — "Water?" —
 Beg your parding, young man, there you lied!

It was *gold*, — in the quartz,
 And it ran all alike;
And I reckon five oughts
 Was the worth of that strike;

And that house with the coopilow 's his'n, — which
the same is n't bad for a Pike.

Thet 's why it 's Dow's Flat ;
And the thing of it is
That he kinder got that
Through sheer contrairiness :
For 't was *water* the derned cuss was seekin', and
his luck made him certain to miss.

Thet 's so. Thar 's your way
To the left of yon tree ;
But — a — look h'yur, say ?
Won't you come up to tea ?
No ? Well, then the next time you 're passin' ; and
ask after Dow, — and thet 's *me.*

IN THE TUNNEL.

DID n't know Flynn, —
 Flynn of Virginia, —
Long as he 's been 'yar?
Look 'ee here, stranger,
Whar *hev* you been?

Here in this tunnel
 He was my pardner,
That same Tom Flynn, —
 Working together,
 In wind and weather,
Day out and in.

Did n't know Flynn!
  Well, that *is* queer;
Why, it 's a sin
To think of Tom Flynn, —
  Tom with his cheer,
  Tom without fear, —
  Stranger, look 'yar!

Thar in the drift,
  Back to the wall,
He held the timbers
  Ready to fall;
  Then in the darkness
I heard him call:
  "Run for your life, Jake!
  Run for your wife's sake!
  Don't wait for me."

And that was all
  Heard in the din,
  Heard of Tom Flynn, —
    Flynn of Virginia.

That 's all about
  Flynn of Virginia.
That lets me out.
  Here in the damp, —
Out of the sun, —
  That 'ar derned lamp
Makes my eyes run.
Well, there, — I 'm done!

But, sir, when you 'll
Hear the next fool
  Asking of Flynn, —

Flynn of Virginia, —
  Just you chip in,
  Say you knew Flynn;
Say that you 've been 'yar.

"CICELY."

ALKALI STATION.

CICELY says you 're a poet; maybe; I ain't much on rhyme:
I reckon you 'd give me a hundred, and beat me every time.
Poetry! — that 's the way some chaps puts up an idee,
But I takes mine "straight without sugar," and that 's what 's the matter with me.

Poetry! — just look round you, — alkali, rock, and sage;
Sage-brush, rock, and alkali; ain't it a pretty page!

Sun in the east at mornin', sun in the west at night,
And the shadow of this 'yer station the on'y thing moves in sight.

Poetry! — Well now — Polly! Polly, run to your mam;
Run right away, my pooty! By by! Ain't she a lamb?
Poetry! — that reminds me o' suthin' right in that suit:
Jest shet that door thar, will yer? — for Cicely's ears is cute.

Ye noticed Polly, — the baby? A month afore she was born,
Cicely — my old woman — was moody-like and forlorn;

Out of her head and crazy, and talked of flowers
and trees;
Family man yourself, sir? Well, you know what
a woman be's.

Narvous she was, and restless, — said that she
"could n't stay."
Stay, — and the nearest woman seventeen miles
away.
But I fixed it up with the doctor, and he said he
would be on hand,
And I kinder stuck by the shanty, and fenced in
that bit o' land.

One night, — the tenth of October, — I woke with
a chill and fright,
For the door it was standing open, and Cicely
warn't in sight,

But a note was pinned on the blanket, which it
said that she "could n't stay,"
But had gone to visit her neighbor, — seventeen
miles away!

When and how she stampeded, I did n't wait for
to see,
For out in the road, next minit, I started as wild
as she;
Running first this way and that way, like a hound
that is off the scent,
For there warn't no track in the darkness to tell
me the way she went.

I 've had some mighty mean moments afore I kem
to this spot, —
Lost on the Plains in '50, drownded almost, and
shot;

But out on this alkali desert, a hunting a crazy
wife,
Was ra'ly as on-satis-factory as anything in my
life.

"Cicely! Cicely! Cicely!" I called, and I held my
breath,
And "Cicely!" came from the canyon,—and all
was as still as death.
And "Cicely! Cicely! Cicely!" came from the
rocks below,
And jest but a whisper of "Cicely!" down from
them peaks of snow.

I ain't what you call religious,—but I jest looked
up to the sky,
And—this 'yer's to what I'm coming, and maybe
ye think I lie:

But up away to the east'ard, yaller and big and far,
I saw of a suddent rising the singlerist kind of star.

Big and yaller and dancing, it seemed to beckon to me:
Yaller and big and dancing, such as you never see:
Big and yaller and dancing, — I never saw such a star,
And I thought of them sharps in the Bible, and I went for it then and thar.

Over the brush and bowlders I stumbled and pushed ahead:
Keeping the star afore me, I went wharever it led.

It might hev been for an hour, when suddent and
peart and nigh,
Out of the yearth afore me thar riz up a baby's
cry.

Listen! thar 's the same music; but her lungs
they are stronger now
Than the day I packed her and her mother,—I 'm
derned if I jest know how.
But the doctor kem the next minit, and the joke
o' the whole thing is
That Cis never knew what happened from that
very night to this!

But Cicely says you 're a poet, and maybe you
might, some day,
Jest sling her a rhyme 'bout a baby that was born
in a curious way.

And see what she says; and, old fellow, when you
speak of the star, don't tell
As how 't was the doctor's lantern, — for maybe
't won't sound so well.

PENELOPE.

SIMPSON'S BAR, 1858.

SO you 've kem 'yer agen,
And one answer won't do?
Well, of all the derned men
That I 've struck, it is you.
O Sal! 'yer 's that derned fool from Simpson's, cavortin' round 'yer in the dew.

Kem in, ef you *will.*
Thar, — quit! Take a cheer.
Not that; you can't fill
Them theer cushings this year, —
For that cheer was my old man's, Joe Simpson, and they don't make such men about 'yer.

He was tall, was my Jack,
And as strong as a tree.
Thar 's his gun on the rack, —
Jest you heft it, and see.
And *you* come a courtin' his widder. Lord! where can that critter, Sal, be!

You 'd fill my Jack's place?
And a man of your size, —
With no baird to his face,
Nor a snap to his eyes, —
And nary — Sho! thar! I was foolin', — I was, Joe, for sartain, — don't rise.

Sit down. Law! why, sho!
I 'm as weak as a gal,

Sal! Don't you go, Joe,
Or I 'll faint, — sure, I shall.
Sit down, — *anywheer*, where you like, Joe, — in that cheer, if you choose, — Lord, where 's Sal!

PLAIN LANGUAGE FROM TRUTHFUL JAMES.

TABLE MOUNTAIN, 1870.

WHICH I wish to remark,—
And my language is plain,—
That for ways that are dark
And for tricks that are vain,
The heathen Chinee is peculiar.
Which the same I would rise to explain.

Ah Sin was his name;
And I shall not deny

In regard to the same
  What that name might imply,
But his smile it was pensive and childlike,
  As I frequent remarked to Bill Nye.

It was August the third ;
  And quite soft was the skies ;
Which it might be inferred
  That Ah Sin was likewise ;
Yet he played it that day upon William
  And me in a way I despise.

Which we had a small game,
  And Ah Sin took a hand :
It was Euchre. The same
  He did not understand ;
But he smiled as he sat by the table,
  With the smile that was childlike and bland.

Yet the cards they were stocked
  In a way that I grieve,
And my feelings were shocked
  At the state of Nye's sleeve:
Which was stuffed full of aces and bowers,
  And the same with intent to deceive.

But the hands that were played
  By that heathen Chinee,
And the points that he made,
  Were quite frightful to see,—
Till at last he put down a right bower,
  Which the same Nye had dealt unto me.

Then I looked up at Nye,
  And he gazed upon me;
And he rose with a sigh,
  And said, "Can this be?

We are ruined by Chinese cheap labor," —
  And he went for that heathen Chinee.

In the scene that ensued
  I did not take a hand,
But the floor it was strewed
  Like the leaves on the strand
With the cards that Ah Sin had been hiding,
  In the game "he did not understand."

In his sleeves, which were long,
  He had twenty-four packs, —
Which was coming it strong,
  Yet I state but the facts;
And we found on his nails, which were taper,
  What is frequent in tapers, — that 's wax.

Which is why I remark,
  And my language is plain,

That for ways that are dark,
  And for tricks that are vain,
The heathen Chinee is peculiar, —
  Which the same I am free to maintain.

THE SOCIETY UPON THE STANISLAUS.

I RESIDE at Table Mountain, and my name is
Truthful James;
I am not up to small deceit, or any sinful games;
And I 'll tell in simple language what I know
about the row
That broke up our society upon the Stanislow.

But first I would remark, that it is not a proper plan
For any scientific gent to whale his fellow-man,
And, if a member don't agree with his peculiar
whim,
To lay for that same member for to "put a head"
on him.

Now nothing could be finer or more beautiful to see
Than the first six months' proceedings of that same society,
Till Brown of Calaveras brought a lot of fossil bones
That he found within a tunnel near the tenement of Jones.

Then Brown he read a paper, and he reconstructed there,
From those same bones, an animal that was extremely rare;
And Jones then asked the Chair for a suspension of the rules,
Till he could prove that those same bones was one of his lost mules.

Then Brown he smiled a bitter smile, and said h
was at fault.
It seemed he had been trespassing on Jones's fan
ily vault:
He was a most sarcastic man, this quiet M
Brown,
And on several occasions he had cleaned out th
town.

Now I hold it is not decent for a scientific gent
To say another is an ass, — at least, to all intent
Nor should the individual who happens to b
meant
Reply by heaving rocks at him to any great e
tent.

Then Abner Dean of Angel's raised a point of c
der — when

A chunk of old red sandstone took him in the
abdomen,
And he smiled a kind of sickly smile, and curled
up on the floor,
And the subsequent proceedings interested him no
more.

For, in less time than I write it, every member
did engage
In a warfare with the remnants of a palæozoic
age;
And the way they heaved those fossils in their
anger was a sin,
Till the skull of an old mammoth caved the head
of Thompson in.

And this is all I have to say of these improper
games,

For I live at Table Mountain, and my name is
Truthful James;
And I 've told in simple language what I know
about the row
That broke up our society upon the Stanislow.

POEMS

FROM 1860 TO 1868.

JOHN BURNS OF GETTYSBURG.

HAVE you heard the story that gossips tell
Of Burns of Gettysburg? — No? Ah, well:
Brief is the glory that hero earns,
Briefer the story of poor John Burns:
He was the fellow who won renown, —
The only man who did n't back down
When the rebels rode through his native town:
But held his own in the fight next day,
When all his townsfolk ran away.
That was in July, sixty-three,
The very day that General Lee,
Flower of Southern chivalry,
Baffled and beaten, backward reeled
From a stubborn Meade and a barren field.

I might tell how, but the day before,
John Burns stood at his cottage door,
Looking down the village street,
Where, in the shade of his peaceful vine,
He heard the low of his gathered kine,
And felt their breath with incense sweet;
Or I might say, when the sunset burned
The old farm gable, he thought it turned
The milk that fell, in a babbling flood
Into the milk-pail, red as blood!
Or how he fancied the hum of bees
Were bullets buzzing among the trees.
But all such fanciful thoughts as these
Were strange to a practical man like Burns,
Who minded only his own concerns,
Troubled no more by fancies fine
Than one of his calm-eyed, long-tailed kine, —

Quite old-fashioned and matter-of-fact,
Slow to argue, but quick to act.
That was the reason, as some folk say,
He fought so well on that terrible day.

And it was terrible. On the right
Raged for hours the heady fight,
Thundered the battery's double bass, —
Difficult music for men to face;
While on the left — where now the graves
Undulate like the living waves
That all that day unceasing swept
Up to the pits the rebels kept —
Round shot ploughed the upland glades,
Sown with bullets, reaped with blades;
Shattered fences here and there
Tossed their splinters in the air;

The very trees were stripped and bare;
The barns that once held yellow grain
Were heaped with harvests of the slain;
The cattle bellowed on the plain,
The turkeys screamed with might and main,
And brooding barn-fowl left their rest
With strange shells bursting in each nest.

Just where the tide of battle turns,
Erect and lonely stood old John Burns.
How do you think the man was dressed?
He wore an ancient long buff vest,
Yellow as saffron, — but his best;
And, buttoned over his manly breast,
Was a bright blue coat, with a rolling collar,
And large gilt buttons, — size of a dollar, —
With tails that the country-folk called "swaller."

He wore a broad-brimmed, bell-crowned hat,
White as the locks on which it sat.
Never had such a sight been seen
For forty years on the village green,
Since old John Burns was a country beau,
And went to the "quiltings" long ago.

Close at his elbows all that day,
Veterans of the Peninsula,
Sunburnt and bearded, charged away;
And striplings, downy of lip and chin, —
Clerks that the Home Guard mustered in, —
Glanced, as they passed, at the hat he wore,
Then at the rifle his right hand bore;
And hailed him, from out their youthful lore,
With scraps of a slangy *répertoire:*
"How are you, White Hat!" "Put her through!"

"Your head 's level," and "Bully for you!"
Called him "Daddy," — begged he 'd disclose
The name of the tailor who made his clothes,
And what was the value he set on those;
While Burns, unmindful of jeer and scoff,
Stood there picking the rebels off, —
With his long brown rifle, and bell-crown hat,
And the swallow-tails they were laughing at.

'T was but a moment, for that respect
Which clothes all courage their voices checked;
And something the wildest could understand
Spake in the old man's strong right hand;
And his corded throat, and the lurking frown
Of his eyebrows under his old bell-crown;
Until, as they gazed, there crept an awe
Through the ranks in whispers, and some men saw,

In the antique vestments and long white hair,
The Past of the Nation in battle there;
And some of the soldiers since declare
That the gleam of his old white hat afar,
Like the crested plume of the brave Navarre,
That day was their oriflamme of war.

So raged the battle. You know the rest:
How the rebels, beaten and backward pressed,
Broke at the final charge, and ran.
At which John Burns — a practical man —
Shouldered his rifle, unbent his brows,
And then went back to his bees and cows.

That is the story of old John Burns;
This is the moral the reader learns:
In fighting the battle, the question 's whether
You 'll show a hat that 's white, or a feather!

THE TALE OF A PONY.

NAME of my heroine, simply "Rose";
Surname, tolerable only in prose;
Habitat, Paris, — that is where
She resided for change of air;
Ætat xx; complexion fair,
Rich, good-looking, and *débonnaire*,
Smarter than Jersey-lightning — There!
That 's her photograph, done with care.

In Paris, whatever they do besides,
EVERY LADY IN FULL DRESS RIDES!
Moire antiques you never meet
Sweeping the filth of a dirty street;

But every woman's claim to *ton*
    Depends upon
The team she drives, whether phaeton,
Landau, or britzka. Hence it 's plain
That Rose, who was of her toilet vain,
Should have a team that ought to be
Equal to any in all *Paris!*

"Bring forth the horse!" — The *commissaire*
Bowed, and brought Miss Rose a pair
Leading an equipage rich and rare:
"Why doth that lovely lady stare?"
Why? The tail of the off gray mare
Is bobbed, — by all that 's good and fair!
Like the shaving-brushes that soldiers wear,
Scarcely showing as much back-hair
As Tam O'Shanter's "Meg," — and there
Lord knows she 'd little enough to spare.

That stare and frown the Frenchman knew,
But did, — as well-bred Frenchmen do:
Raised his shoulders above his crown,
Joined his thumbs, with the fingers down,
And said, "Ah Heaven!" — then, "Mademoiselle,
Delay one minute, and all is well!"
He went; returned; by what good chance
These things are managed so well in France
I cannot say, — but he made the sale,
And the bob-tailed mare had a flowing tail.

All that is false in this world below
Betrays itself in a love of show;
Indignant Nature hides her lash
In the purple-black of a dyed mustache;
The shallowest fop will trip in French,
The would-be critic will misquote Trench;

In short, you 're always sure to detect
A sham in the things folks most affect;
Bean-pods are noisiest when dry,
And you always wink with your weakest eye:
And that 's the reason the old gray mare
Forever had her tail in the air,
With flourishes beyond compare,
        Though every whisk
        Incurred the risk
Of leaving that sensitive region bare, —
She did some things that you could n't but feel
She would n't have done had her tail been real.

Champs Elysées: Time, past five;
There go the carriages, — look alive!
Everything that man can drive,
Or his inventive skill contrive, —

Yankee buggy or English "chay";
Dog-cart, droschky, and smart coupé,
A *désoblijeante* quite bulky,
(French idea of a Yankee *sulky;*)
Band in the distance, playing a march,
Footmen standing stiff as starch;
Savans, lorettes, deputies, Arch-
Bishops, and there together range
Sous-lieutenants and *cent*-gardes, (strange
Way these soldier-chaps make change,)
Mixed with black-eyed Polish dames,
With unpronounceable awful names;
Laces tremble, and ribbons flout,
Coachmen wrangle and gendarmes shout,—
Bless us! what is the row about?
Ah! here comes Rosey's new turn-out!

Smart! You bet your life 't was that!
Nifty! (short for *magnificat*)
Mulberry panels, — heraldic spread, —
Ebony wheels picked out with red,
And two gray mares that were thoroughbred;
No wonder that every dandy's head
Was turned by the turn-out, — and 't was said
That Caskowhisky (friend of the Czar),
A very good *whip* (as Russians are),
Was tied to Rosey's triumphal car,
Entranced, the reader will understand,
By "ribbons" that graced her head and hand.

Alas! the hour you think would crown
Your highest wishes should let you down!
Or Fate should turn, by your own mischance,
Your victor's car to an ambulance;

From cloudless heavens her lightnings glance,
(And these things happen, even in France ;)
And so Miss Rose, as she trotted by, —
The cynosure of every eye, —
Saw to her horror the off mare shy, —
Flourish her tail so exceeding high
That, disregarding the closest tie,
And without giving a reason why,
She flung that tail so free and frisky
Off in the face of Caskowhisky!

Excuses, blushes, smiles: in fine,
End of the pony's tail, and mine!

THE MIRACLE OF PADRE JUNIPERO.

THIS is the tale that the Chronicle
Tells of the wonderful miracle
Wrought by the pious Padre Serro,
The very reverend Junipero.

The Heathen stood on his ancient mound,
Looking over the desert bound
Into the distant, hazy south,
Over the dusty and broad champaign
Where, with many a gaping mouth,
And fissure cracked by the fervid drouth,

5*

For seven months had the wasted plain
Known no moisture of dew or rain.
The wells were empty and choked with sand;
The rivers had perished from the land;
Only the sea fogs, to and fro,
Slipped like ghosts of the streams below.
Deep in its bed lay the river's bones,
Bleaching in pebbles and milk-white stones,
And tracked o'er the desert faint and far,
Its ribs shone bright on each sandy bar.

Thus they stood as the sun went down
Over the foot-hills bare and brown;
Thus they looked to the South, wherefrom
The pale-face medicine-man should come.
Not in anger, or in strife,
But to bring — so ran the tale —

The welcome springs of eternal life,
The living waters that should not fail.

Said one, "He will come like Manitou,
Unseen, unheard, in the falling dew."
Said another, "He will come full soon
Out of the round-faced watery moon."
And another said, "He is here!" and lo,—
Faltering, staggering, feeble and slow,—
Out from the desert's blinding heat
The Padre dropped at the heathen's feet.
They stood and gazed for a little space
Down on his pallid and careworn face,
And a smile of scorn went round the band
As they touched alternate with foot and hand
This mortal waif, that the outer space
Of dim mysterious sky and sand

Flung with so little of Christian grace
Down on their barren, sterile strand.

Said one to him: "It seems thy god
Is a very pitiful kind of god;
He could not shield thine aching eyes
From the blowing desert sands that rise,
Nor turn aside from thy old gray head
The glittering blade that is brandishéd
By the sun he set in the heavens high;
He could not moisten thy lips when dry;
The desert fire is in thy brain;
Thy limbs are racked with the fever-pain:
If this be the grace he showeth thee
Who art his servant, what may we,
Strange to his ways and his commands,
Seek at his unforgiving hands?"

"Drink but this cup," said the Padre, straight,
"And thou shalt know whose mercy bore
These aching limbs to your heathen door,
And purged my soul of its gross estate.
Drink in His name, and thou shalt see
The hidden depths of this mystery.
Drink!" and he held the cup. One blow
From the heathen dashed to the ground below
The sacred cup that the Padre bore;
And the thirsty soil drank the precious store
Of sacramental and holy wine,
That emblem and consecrated sign
And blessed symbol of blood divine.

Then, says the legend, (and they who doubt
The same as heretics be accurst,)
From the dry and feverish soil leaped out

A living fountain; a well-spring burst
Over the dusty and broad champaign,
Over the sandy and sterile plain,
Till the granite ribs and the milk-white stones
That lay in the valley — the scattered bones —
Moved in the river and lived again!

Such was the wonderful miracle
Wrought by the cup of wine that fell
From the hands of the pious Padre Serro,
The very reverend Junipero.

AN ARCTIC VISION.

WHERE the short-legged Esquimaux
Waddle in the ice and snow,
And the playful polar bear
Nips the hunter unaware;
Where by day they track the ermine,
And by night another vermin, —
Segment of the frigid zone,
Where the temperature alone
Warms on St. Elias' cone;
Polar dock, where Nature slips
From the ways her icy ships;
Land of fox and deer and sable,

Shore end of our western cable,—
Let the news that flying goes
Thrill through all your Arctic floes,
And reverberate the boast
From the cliffs of Beechey's coast,
Till the tidings, circling round
Every bay of Norton Sound,
Throw the vocal tide-wave back
To the isles of Kodiac.
Let the stately polar bears
Waltz around the pole in pairs,
And the walrus, in his glee,
Bare his tusk of ivory;
While the bold sea unicorn
Calmly takes an extra horn;
All ye polar skies, reveal your
Very rarest of parhelia;

Trip it, all ye merry dancers,
In the airiest of lancers;
Slide, ye solemn glaciers, slide,
One inch farther to the tide,
Nor in rash precipitation
Upset Tyndall's calculation.
Know you not what fate awaits you,
Or to whom the future mates you?
All ye icebergs make salaam, —
You belong to Uncle Sam!

On the spot where Eugene Sue
Led his wretched Wandering Jew,
Stands a form whose features strike
Russ and Esquimaux alike.
He it is whom Skalds of old
In their Runic rhymes foretold;

Lean of flank and lank of jaw,
See the real Northern Thor!
See the awful Yankee leering
Just across the Straits of Behring;
On the drifted snow, too plain,
Sinks his fresh tobacco stain
Just beside the deep inden-
Tation of his Number 10.

Leaning on his icy hammer
Stands the hero of this drama,
And above the wild-duck's clamor,
In his own peculiar grammar,
With its linguistic disguises,
Lo, the Arctic prologue rises:
"Wa'll, I reckon 't ain't so bad,
Seein' ez 't was all they had;

True, the Springs are rather late
And early Falls predominate;
But the ice crop 's pretty sure,
And the air is kind o' pure;
'T aint so very mean a trade,
When the land is all surveyed.
There 's a right smart chance for fur-chase
All along this recent purchase,
And, unless the stories fail,
Every fish from cod to whale;
Rocks, too; mebbe quartz; let 's see, —
'T would be strange if there should be, —
Seems I 've heerd such stories told;
Eh! — why, bless us, — yes, it 's gold!"

While the blows are falling thick
From his California pick,

You may recognize the Thor
Of the vision that I saw, —
Freed from legendary glamour,
See the real magician's hammer.

TO THE PLIOCENE SKULL.

A GEOLOGICAL ADDRESS.

"SPEAK, O man, less recent! Fragmentary fossil!
Primal pioneer of pliocene formation,
Hid in lowest drifts below the earliest stratum
Of volcanic tufa!

"Older than the beasts, the oldest Palæotherium;
Older than the trees, the oldest Cryptogami;
Older than the hills, those infantile eruptions
Of earth's epidermis!

"Eo — Mio — Plio — whatsoe'er the "cene" was
That those vacant sockets filled with awe and
wonder, —

Whether shores Devonian or Silurian beaches,—
Tell us thy strange story!

"Or has the professor slightly antedated
By some thousand years thy advent on this planet,
Giving thee an air that 's somewhat better fitted
For cold-blooded creatures?

"Wert thou true spectator of that mighty forest
When above thy head the stately Sigillaria
Reared its columned trunks in that remote and distant
Carboniferous epoch?

"Tell us of that scene,—the dim and watery woodland
Songless, silent, hushed, with never bird or insect
Veiled with spreading fronds and screened with tall club-mosses,
Lycopodiacea,—

"When beside thee walked the solemn Plesiosaurus,
And around thee crept the festive Ichthyosaurus,
While from time to time above thee flew and circled
Cheerful Pterodactyls.

"Tell us of thy food, — those half-marine refections,
Crinoids on the shell and Brachipods *au naturel*, —
Cuttle-fish to which the *pieuvre* of Victor Hugo
Seems a periwinkle.

"Speak, thou awful vestige of the Earth's creation, —
Solitary fragment of remains organic!
Tell the wondrous secret of thy past existence, —
Speak! thou oldest primate!"

Even as I gazed, a thrill of the maxilla,
And a lateral movement of the condyloid process,

With post-pliocene sounds of healthy mastication,
Ground the teeth together.

And, from that imperfect dental exhibition,
Stained with expressed juices of the weed Nicotian,
Came these hollow accents, blent with softer murmurs
Of expectoration ;

"Which my name is Bowers, and my crust was busted
Falling down a shaft in Calaveras County,
But I 'd take it kindly if you 'd send the pieces
Home to old Missouri!"

THE BALLAD OF THE EMEU.

O SAY, have you seen at the Willows so green,—
So charming and rurally true,—
A singular bird, with a manner absurd,
Which they call the Australian Emeu?
Have you
Ever seen this Australian Emeu?

It trots all around with its head on the ground,
Or erects it quite out of your view;
And the ladies all cry, when its figure they spy,
O, what a sweet pretty Emeu!
Oh! do
Just look at that lovely Emeu!

One day to this spot, when the weather was hot,
Came Matilda Hortense Fortescue;
And beside her there came a youth of high name, —
Augustus Florell Montague:
The two
Both loved that wild, foreign Emeu.

With two loaves of bread then they fed it, instead
Of the flesh of the white cockatoo,
Which once was its food in that wild neighborhood
Where ranges the sweet Kangaroo;
That too
Is game for the famous Emeu!

Old saws and gimlets but its appetite whets
Like the world-famous bark of Peru;
There 's nothing so hard that the bird will discard,

And nothing its taste will eschew,
That you
Can give that long-legged Emeu!

The time slipped away in this innocent play,
When up jumped the bold Montague:
"Where 's that specimen pin that I gayly did win
In raffle, and gave unto you,
Fortescue?"
No word spoke the guilty Emeu!

"Quick! tell me his name whom thou gavest that same,
Ere these hands in thy blood I imbrue!"
"Nay, dearest," she cried, as she clung to his side,
"I 'm innocent as that Emeu!"
"Adieu!"
He replied, "Miss M. H. Fortescue!"

Down she dropped at his feet, all as white as a sheet,
 As wildly he fled from her view;
He thought 't was her sin, — for he knew not the pin
 Had been gobbled up by the Emeu;
 All through
 The voracity of that Emeu!

THE AGED STRANGER.

AN INCIDENT OF THE WAR.

"I WAS with Grant —" the stranger said;
Said the farmer, "Say no more,
But rest thee here at my cottage porch,
For thy feet are weary and sore."

"I was with Grant —" the stranger said;
Said the farmer, "Nay, no more, —
I prithee sit at my frugal board,
And eat of my humble store.

"How fares my boy, — my soldier boy,
Of the old Ninth Army Corps?

I warrant he bore him gallantly
  In the smoke and the battle's roar!"

"I know him not," said the aged man,
  "And, as I remarked before,
I was with Grant —" "Nay, nay, I know,"
  Said the farmer, "say no more;

"He fell in battle, — I see, alas!
  Thou 'dst smooth these tidings o'er, —
Nay: speak the truth, whatever it be,
  Though it rend my bosom's core.

"How fell he, — with his face to the foe,
  Upholding the flag he bore?
O, say not that my boy disgraced
  The uniform that he wore!"

"I cannot tell," said the aged man,
  "And should have remarked, before,
That I was with Grant, — in Illinois, —
  Some three years before the war."

Then the farmer spake him never a word,
  But beat with his fist full sore
That aged man, who had worked for Grant
  Some three years before the war.

"HOW ARE YOU, SANITARY?"

DOWN the picket-guarded lane,
Rolled the comfort-laden wain,
Cheered by shouts that shook the plain,
Soldier-like and merry:
Phrases such as camps may teach,
Sabre-cuts of Saxon speech,
Such as "Bully!" "Them 's the peach!"
"Wade in, Sanitary!"

Right and left the caissons drew,
As the car went lumbering through,
Quick succeeding in review
Squadrons military;

Sunburnt men with beards like frieze,
Smooth-faced boys, and cries like these,—
"U. S. San. Com." "That 's the cheese!"
    "Pass in, Sanitary!"

In such cheer it struggled on
Till the battle front was won,
Then the car, its journey done,
    Lo! was stationary;
And where bullets whistling fly,
Came the sadder, fainter cry,
"Help us, brothers, ere we die,—
    Save us, Sanitary!"

Such the work. The phantom flies,
Wrapped in battle clouds that rise;
But the brave — whose dying eyes,
    Veiled and visionary,

See the jasper gates swung wide,
See the parted throng outside—
Hears the voice to those who ride·
"Pass in, Sanitary!"

THE REVEILLE.

HARK! I hear the tramp of thousands,
  And of armèd men the hum;
Lo! a nation's hosts have gathered
  Round the quick alarming drum, —
    Saying, "Come,
    Freemen, come!
Ere your heritage be wasted," said the quick alarming drum.

"Let me of my heart take counsel:
  War is not of Life the sum;
Who shall stay and reap the harvest
  When the autumn days shall come?"

But the drum
Echoed, "Come!
Death shall reap the braver harvest," said the solemn-sounding drum.

"But when won the coming battle,
What of profit springs therefrom?
What if conquest, subjugation,
Even greater ills become?"
But the drum
Answered, "Come!
You must do the sum to prove it," said the Yankee-answering drum.

"What if, 'mid the cannons' thunder,
Whistling shot and bursting bomb,
When my brothers fall around me,
Should my heart grow cold and numb?"

But the drum
Answered "Come!
Better there in death united, than in life a recreant, — come!"

Thus they answered, — hoping, fearing,
Some in faith, and doubting some,
Till a trumpet-voice proclaiming,
Said, "My chosen people, come!"
Then the drum,
Lo! was dumb,
For the great heart of the nation, throbbing, answered, "Lord, we come!"

OUR PRIVILEGE.

NOT ours, where battle smoke upcurls,
And battle dews lie wet,
To meet the charge that treason hurls
By sword and bayonet.

Not ours to guide the fatal scythe
The fleshless reaper wields;
The harvest moon looks calmly down
Upon our peaceful fields.

The long grass dimples on the hill,
The pines sing by the sea,

And Plenty, from her golden horn,
  Is pouring far and free.

O brothers by the farther sea,
  Think still our faith is warm;
The same bright flag above us waves
  That swathed our baby form.

The same red blood that dyes your fields
  Here throbs in patriot pride;
The blood that flowed when Lander fell,
  And Baker's crimson tide.

And thus apart our hearts keep time
  With every pulse ye feel,
And Mercy's ringing gold shall chime
  With Valor's clashing steel.

RELIEVING GUARD.

T. S. K. OBIIT MARCH 4, 1864.

CAME the Relief. "What, Sentry, ho!
How passed the night through thy long waking?"
"Cold, cheerless, dark, — as may befit
The hour before the dawn is breaking."

"No sight? no sound?" "No; nothing save
The plover from the marshes calling,
And in yon Western sky, about
An hour ago, a Star was falling."

"A star? There's nothing strange in that."
"No, nothing; but, above the thicket,
Somehow it seemed to me that God
Somewhere had just relieved a picket."

PARODIES.

A GEOLOGICAL MADRIGAL.

AFTER HERRICK.

I HAVE found out a gift for my fair;
I know where the fossils abound,
Where the footprints of *Aves* declare
The birds that once walked on the ground;
O, come, and — in technical speech —
We 'll walk this Devonian shore,
Or on some Silurian beach
We 'll wander, my love, evermore.

I will show thee the sinuous track
By the slow-moving annelid made,

Or the Trilobite that, farther back,
  In the old Potsdam sandstone was laid
Thou shalt see, in his Jurassic tomb,
  The Plesiosaurus embalmed;
In his Oolitic prime and his bloom, —
  Iguanodon safe and unharmed!

You wished — I remember it well,
  And I loved you the more for that wish —
For a perfect cystedian shell
  And a *whole* holocephalic fish.
And O, if Earth's strata contains
  In its lowest Silurian drift,
Or Palæozoic remains
  The same, — 't is your lover's free gift!

Then come, love, and never say nay,
  But calm all your maidenly fears,

We 'll note, love, in one summer's day
  The record of millions of years;
And though the Darwinian plan
  Your sensitive feelings may shock,
We 'll find the beginning of man, —
  Our fossil ancestors in rock!

THE WILLOWS.

AFTER EDGAR A. POE.

THE skies they were ashen and sober,
The streets they were dirty and drear;
It was night in the month of October,
Of my most immemorial year;
Like the skies I was perfectly sober,
As I stopped at the mansion of Shear, —
At the Nightingale, — perfectly sober,
And the willowy woodland, down here.

Here, once in an alley Titanic
Of Ten-pins, — I roamed with my soul, —
Of Ten-pins, — with Mary, my soul;

They were days when my heart was volcanic,
  And impelled me to frequently roll,
  And made me resistlessly roll,
Till my ten-strikes created a panic
  In the realms of the Boreal pole,
Till my ten-strikes created a panic
  With the monkey atop of his pole.

I repeat, I was perfectly sober,
  But my thoughts they were palsied and sear,—
  My thoughts were decidedly queer;
For I knew not the month was October,
  And I marked not the night of the year;
I forgot that sweet *morceau* of Auber
  That the band oft performéd down here,
And I mixed the sweet music of Auber
  With the Nightingale's music by Shear.

And now as the night was senescent,
  And star-dials pointed to morn,
  And car-drivers hinted of morn,
At the end of the path a liquescent
  And bibulous lustre was born;
'T was made by the bar-keeper present,
  Who mixéd a duplicate horn,—
His two hands describing a crescent
  Distinct with a duplicate horn.

And I said: "This looks perfectly regal,
  For it 's warm, and I know I feel dry,—
  I am confident that I feel dry;
We have come past the emeu and eagle,
  And watched the gay monkey on high;
Let us drink to the emeu and eagle,—
  To the swan and the monkey on high —

To the eagle and monkey on high;
For this barkeeper will not inveigle,—
Bully boy with the vitreous eye;
He surely would never inveigle,—
Sweet youth with the crystalline eye."

But Mary, uplifting her finger,
Said, "Sadly this bar I mistrust,—
I fear that this bar does not trust.
O hasten! O let us not linger!
O fly,—let us fly,—ere we must!"
In terror she cried, letting sink her
Parasol till it trailed in the dust,—
In agony sobbed, letting sink her
Parasol till it trailed in the dust,—
Till it sorrowfully trailed in the dust.

Then I pacified Mary and kissed her,
  And tempted her into the room,
  And conquered her scruples and gloom ;
And we passed to the end of the vista,
  But were stopped by the warning of doom, —
  By some words that were warning of doom.
And I said, "What is written, sweet sister,
  At the opposite end of the room ?"
She sobbed, as she answered, "All liquors
  Must be paid for ere leaving the room."

Then my heart it grew ashen and sober,
  As the streets were deserted and drear, —
  For my pockets were empty and drear ;
And I cried, "It was surely October,
  On this very night of last year,
  That I journeyed — I journeyed down here, —

That I brought a fair maiden down here,
On this night of all nights in the year.
Ah! to me that inscription is clear;
Well I know now, I 'm perfectly sober,
Why no longer they credit me here, —
Well I know now that music of Auber,
And this Nightingale, kept by one Shear.

NORTH BEACH.

AFTER SPENSER.

LO! where the castle of bold Pfeiffer throws
Its sullen shadow on the rolling tide, —
No more the home where joy and wealth repose,
But now where wassailers in cells abide;
See yon long quay that stretches far and wide,
Well known to citizens as wharf of Meiggs;
There each sweet Sabbath walks in maiden pride
The pensive Margaret, and brave Pat, whose legs
Encased in broadcloth oft keep time with Peg's.

Here cometh oft the tender nursery-maid,
While in her ear her love his tale doth pour;

Meantime her infant doth her charge evade,
And rambleth sagely on the sandy shore,
Till the sly sea-crab, low in ambush laid,
Seizeth his leg and biteth him full sore.
Ah me! what sounds the shuddering echoes bore,
When his small treble mixed with Ocean's roar.

Hard by there stands an ancient hostelrie,
And at its side a garden, where the bear,
The stealthy catamount, and coon agree
To work deceit on all who gather there;
And when Augusta — that unconscious fair —
With nuts and apples plieth Bruin free,
Lo! the green parrot claweth her back hair,
And the gray monkey grabbeth fruits that she
On her gay bonnet wears, and laugheth loud in glee!

THE LOST TAILS OF MILETUS.

HIGH on the Thracian hills, half hid in the billows of clover,
Thyme, and the asphodel blooms, and lulled by Pactolian streamlet,
She of Miletus lay, and beside her an aged satyr
Scratched his ear with his hoof, and playfully mumbled his chestnuts.

Vainly the Mænid and the Bassarid gambolled about her,
The free-eyed Bacchante sang, and Pan — the renowned, the accomplished —

Executed his difficult solo. In vain were their
gambols and dances:
High o'er the Thracian hills rose the voice of the
shepherdess, wailing.

"Ai! for the fleecy flocks, — the meek-nosed, the
passionless faces;
Ai! for the tallow-scented, the straight-tailed, the
high-stepping;
Ai! for the timid glance, which is that which the
rustic, sagacious,
Applies to him who loves but may not declare his
passion!"

Her then Zeus answered slow: "O daughter of
song and sorrow, —
Hapless tender of sheep, — arise from thy long lam-
entation!

Since thou canst not trust fate, nor behave as becomes a Greek maiden,
Look and behold thy sheep." — And lo! they returned to her tailless!

THE END.

Cambridge: Electrotyped and Printed by Welch, Bigelow, & Co.